Energy for Christians

Words of Wisdom, Prayers and Insightful Sayings

Roy Lee Williams

WESTBOW
P R E S S®
A DIVISION OF THOMAS NELSON
& ZONDERVAN

WestBow Press books may be ordered through booksellers or by contacting:

WestBow Press
A Division of Thomas Nelson & Zondervan
1663 Liberty Drive
Bloomington, IN 47403
www.westbowpress.com
844-714-3454

ISBN: 978-1-6642-8379-4 (sc)
ISBN: 978-1-6642-8380-0 (e)

Library of Congress Control Number: 2022921177

Print information available on the last page.

WestBow Press rev. date: 12/13/2022

Contents

Prayer

Prayer Diary

Acknowledgement

A very special thanks to my Wife Laverne E. Williams for her unwavering encouragement and support throughout this entire process. Additionally, to the Body of Christ Church family at large, and especially my Grandchildren for being a source of inspiration thank You ALL.

Category:

_____

Admonish

Be courageous in Fighting for Your VICTORY.

Belief should be shared and not imposed.

Don't be a victim of blindness.

Don't be a victim to behavioral manipulation.

Don't be a victim to lack of faith.

Don't choke on Pride seek wisdom.

Don't let negativity capture your mind.

Don't let your Victory be overturned.

Don't stay in wrongdoing but move into right doing.

Do the right thing not because you must but because it is the right thing to do!

Have compassion.

Listen for Jesus voice today.

Respect Leadership.

Take a stance.

Teaching should be done with wisdom not with fear.

Teaching should be done with wisdom not intimidation.

Upward, downward and all around disconnect from Evil.

Walk in God.

You have spoken it Now Do It.

Category:

_____

Advice

Attend a worship service and let the Holy Spirit renew your Joy.

Before you need one be one - a good friend.

Change Your Path.

Don't be a tool to behavioral manipulation.

Don't ignore what is TRUE; Evil and evil speech are real.

Don't ignore what you heard hate and mass murders are real.

Do right because it is the right thing to do not because you must.

Give God your best.

Give God your heart.

God loves all people, but man hate people that are different.

Hear, believe and respond.

Jumpstart your faith.

Respect and cherish good Leadership.

Learn to discipline yourself by self-denial at least once a week for 12 hours.

Recharge Your Faith.

Remain focused don't be distracted.

Remember what you said you would never forget.

Resist evil, not progress.

Trust God.

Trust in Hope and Wait.

Stay alert.

Category:

_____

Awareness

Analyst, commentators, Seers, Prophets, have all declared and yet your future is in the hands of God.

Faith is Power.

From your eternal life insurance specialist purchase death insurance.

God's silence isn't Abandonment.

Identify division makers and unity Fighters.

It is natural to go from innocent to self-aware to sin, but it is spiritual to be converted.

Remember what has been Forgotten.

See Division and Understand Division.

Some accept Mercy through the cross, but some don't.

Stay focused and shut out he said she said gossip.

The world has a Savior and everyone needs to align with Christ the Savior.

There is no change in the wrong done because of who exposes it.

There is a huge difference in knowing Christ and only knowing about Christ.

Things you thought would give you happiness don't.

Understand how you got where you are.

Your choice; choose godliness or sin.

Your choice; choose life or death.

Your choice; Freedom or addiction.

Your choice is your choice when with freedom it is made.

Your choice; choose righteousness or pleasure.

Category:

Blessed

Christ Jesus is the gift for everyone.

Despite maneuvers and strategies designed to stop my success I am still blessed.

Father God is our helper.

From Heaven is Flowing Showers of Blessings get your bucket.

God's blessings are available in abundance.

God's goodness is available in abundance.

Heaven's window is open with love, grace and mercy flowing.

It's a blessing to walk with God.

Eternal Life is a promise to You.

We are children of God through Faith.

Category:

_____

Boldness

If good people see evil and do nothing, then evil people will continue to do evil.

Jesus Christ showed the world with Love and his disciples are required to do the same.

Sharing is spreading the good news.

Speak truth about a lie.

Stand confident in struggle.

Take a stance.

Talk Faith and Walk Faithfully.

Testify about God.

Gaining Victory requires fighting with Faith.

We can't be defeated when allowing Christ to direct out Steps.

Category:

_____

Comfort

Bad things happen to good people, but God our Father controls our reward.

Christ Jesus is our great liberator and emancipator.

During tragic and devastating times, you can find comfort in Christ Jesus.

Help is already dispatched with your name on it.

In our night moment Jesus will come through.

Jesus Christ will give you Joy in sadness.

Let the Holy Spirit comfort you in sadness.

Stay calm there's no destruction in your storm.

The Illuminating Light of Christ is ever shining bright leading Believers through the darkness of night.

Grace is available to all Humanity.

Category:

_____

Counseling

Before seeking professional counseling seek God for He is our counselor.

Change Your Path.

Don't cheat God and then ask Him to bless you.

Don't give a seat to negativity at the table of your mind.

Don't just accept any word you get but get the word God has for you.

Do right not because you are forced to but because it's the right thing to do.

Let God counsel you and welcome His guidance.

Plug-in forgiveness.

Resist evil.

Stop waiting and start accepting.

Turn your worries over to God our Father.

Wash your mind with the word of God.

Category:

_____

Declaration

God isn't our private procession we belong to him.

Help is already dispatched with your name on it.

I am a beneficiary of God's goodness.

I am a witness.

I declare victory for myself.

I love Christ Jesus.

I love Father God almighty.

I love God my Savior.

I love the Holy Spirit.

My Success is ordained by God; failure isn't an option.

The greatness of God can't be erased buy evil doers.

Category:

_____

Dedication/Obedience

Don't give up and don't give in.

Know better do better.

Let your yes be yes and your no be no.

Stay focused and stick with the Vision.

Trust In Hope and wait.

Walk in God.

Some believers are willing to engage in self-denial to please you Lord.

Yes Lord, here am I.

Yes Lord, I give you my all.

Yes Lord, I trust you and I will comply.

Category:

Encouragement

Be Resolute and continue to fight the good fight of faith.

Christ the righteous King is fair and Just.

Deliverance is already sent with your name on it.

God Cares.

God our father he is a keeper and sustainer.

It's not done until God says it's done.

Stand strong for righteousness' sake.

Stay Focus Victory is ahead.

The door to your freedom is open walk through it.

We are more than conquerors.

Category:

_____

Faith

Believe in God.

Believe Jesus today.

Believe the impossible and God will change your World.

Believe the sign you see and trust the confirmation.

Blind loyalty demands ignoring godliness but being faithful requires trusting in godliness.

Faith Believers walk without seeing a path.

Faith is the currency for miracles.

Faith The Talk and faith the walk.

Let the word of God feed your faith.

Make a choice and walk in it.

Step into your destiny.

See God.

See who causes divisions and who brings about Unity.

Stay focused help others to trust God.

Trust God in all things big and small.

Trust in what you believe not how you feel.

Trust Jesus today.

Trust the Lord in the storm even if you get wet.

Walk by the spirit.

Walk in faith.

Without faith there can be no trust.

Without trust faith is Hollow.

Category:

_____

Grateful

Every day is a day of redemption.

For our Salvation Christ Jesus Paid the cost.

God's love is all inclusive.

In the heart of God is forgiveness.

Remembering what you said you would never forget.

Salvation is personal.

Some of you were hidden from birth.

No one loves me the way Christ does.

Thanks for keeping destructive forces from destroying me.

Thanks for wrapping me in Your Mercy.

Category:

Insight

Absence isn't Abandonment.

Behavioral manipulation is used to control our actions and our reactions.

Behavioral manipulation is used to influence and control your actions.

Christ is the expert for all human life, why listen to anyone else.

Deception by others is very bad but self-deception is worse.

Distractions are meant to redirect our Focus.

God's knowledge is eternal, but man's knowledge becomes obsolete.

Hatred and phobias are products of spiritual Darkness.

Living beneath one's privilege should never become one's norm.

Making a choice can be right or can be wrong.

My goodness isn't determined by what you do.

Neither promotions nor titles change Behavior repentance does.

Ownership isn't Freewill.

Perfect language doesn't automatically interpret to correct interpretation.

Stay focused and understand so-called friends may attempt to block your progress.

Stay focused and understand that in the process there will be some difficulties.

some are determined to be right even in the face undisputable wrong.

Someone is always pouring into your life why not let God.

The highest level in human growth is to treat others as you treat yourself.

Truth is truth regardless of perspective.

Who exposes wrongdoing doesn't change the wrong.

Your choice is your choice when with freedom it is made.

Category:

_____

Instructional

Allow a kind gesture, a kind word or smile be something you share.

Christians are called to be faithful not loyal.

Get to the birthplace of your breakthrough.

Grow in wisdom.

How is God speaking when he isn't heard.

Ideals are seeds that can be planted in the soil of your mind.

If the Lost can't find themselves then who can save the Lost.

Jesus didn't tell sinners to go and cleanse themselves and then come back for salvation.

Learn and know the voice of Jesus Christ.

Learning to love God, loving yourself and loving all People.

Listen for Jesus today.

Pray with your family.

Say yes to Christ the Lord.

Turn away from confusion seek clarity.

Understand why you are where you are.

Walk in the spirit.

Category:

_____

Invitation

Accept God.

Accept God's help!

Come eat from Heaven's Table.

God's spirit is real freely drink from The Well of Living Water.

Hear God.

Share with someone the gift of Christ.

Today can be a new day just asked Jesus for a restart.

Welcome the Holy Spirit let him guide you.

Worshipers sought no experience necessary.

Your choice; accept or deny Christ.

Category:

_____

Love

Belief should be shared lovingly not imposed.

Godly love is all inclusive.

God's love is genuine, authentic and real.

God's love is unconditional.

Hate is a cancer that eats away at love until there isn't any compassion.

No matter what comes upon us we must continue to Love.

Love is passed upward, downward, crossways and all around.

Love yourself first then love others as you Love yourself.

The highest level in human growth is to treat others as you treat yourself and to treat everyone the same.

Unity isn't the absence of differences but the acceptance of differences.

Category:

Motivation/Uplifting

Manifest your hidden treasure.

Stay Focus helping others to trust God.

Today is a day of salvation.

Trusting God should be a way of life.

Victory is in resisting and failure is in surrendering to evil.

Blessings already have your name on them.

Call back to your remembrance what God Promised You.

Goodness wants to Capture You.

Not everyone can help in your time of trouble, but Jesus Christ can.

Today Freedom comes to you.

Wise teachers use wisdom, not fear.

Category:

_____

Power

Activate your own determination it belongs to you.

Some face, some avoid, and some fight but all must overcome temptation.

The holy spirit is a truth detector.

The power God has given is enough.

The spirit of God is our power source.

There's freeing power in knowing the truth.

True righteousness doesn't need justification.

Light is Power.

Good News is a source of strength.

Remain confident waiting for the Outcome in your struggle.

Category:

_____

Praise

After all I've been through, I still love my God and my Savior.

Father God thanks for helping me see your goodness.

Glorify God.

God our Father is a Keeper.

I must testify about God's Goodness.

I'm not only a witness I'm a beneficiary of God's goodness.

Let's celebrate Jesus today in worship.

Praising God is good therapy.

Thank you, Lord Jesus, for being our burden Bearer.

We thank you Father God for allowing us to see this day.

Welcome his presence.

What God has done is enough.

Wear praise like a garment.

Category:

_____

Prayer

Ask God for the word you need to hear.

Bless me and not my enemy.

Father God grant us peace.

Father God increase our faith.

Father God please grant all an open door to Freedom.

Father God thank you for this day you've allowed us to see.

Lord Jesus give me confidence, hope, power and strength.

Open my spiritual eyes and let me see what is before me.

Pray for someone today.

Prayer is our way of communicating with God.

Category:

Sadness

A Godless life is an unfulfilled life!

Don't let your afterlife insurance policy expire.

God's love is race-blind, but man's hate Targets any people!

Jealousy and envy have no place in the church.

Phobias and hatred are products of spiritual Darkness.

Emotional disturbance doesn't live here anymore.

The word of God is my medicine for anxiety.

Loneliness attempts at co-habitation will fail.

Sometimes it is okay to cry.

All my earthly possessions are gone but I still have peace.

Category:

_____

Strength/Togetherness

Fellowship with God is our sanity.

Fighting not to give up.

Just because wrong actions can get desired benefits stand for righteousness.

Stay strong.

Stop doubting and start accepting.

Celebrate differences.

God's Divine Purpose for us is fellowship with him.

Let the Righteous, the Holy, the Truthful and the Good Worship together.

One message on messenger speaking through all by the spirit of God.

There is a renewed call for prayer all over the land seek God.

Unity isn't the absence of difference but the acceptance of differences.

Category:

_____

Troubled/Warning

Don't allow your deliverance to become your bondage.

Don't let negativity capture your mind.

Fighting amongst each other has no place in the church.

Sometimes more isn't enough and sometimes less is too much.

Don't be a tool to behavioral manipulation.

Don't be a victim of behavioral manipulation.

Don't contribute to my darkness of night but bring me light.

Don't let your Victory be overturned.

Overcome fear by accepting the love of Christ.

Your destiny can't be overturned.

Category:

Truth

Every person has history.

For God a promise made is a promise kept.

Heaven's Power is Greatest of All Time (GOAT).

In Christ there is but one People.

No Flesh is Perfect.

Some people choose to lie rather than tell the truth.

Truth is truth regardless of perspective.

For every Sin there is a cost.

Forgiveness is a pillar in Christianity.

Satan isn't a Friend.

Category:

_____

Wisdom

Birth happiness stop living in misery.

Do nothing and nothing will continue to happen do something and something will happen.

Don't Only Break Up with It – Give It Up.

Don't stay in wrongdoing but move into right doing.

Don't try to lead the Holy Spirit.

Everyone should eat "SOUL" FOOD.

I thought my purpose was for me to be in your life now I realize the purpose was for you to be in my life.

Ideas are seeds that are planted in the soil of your mind.

If you deceive others, Others May deceive you.

Love rejoices in success and hatred rejoices in failure.

My life and my existence should be in God.

Our minds are incubators for thoughts good and bad.

Promotion/Titles don't change behavior Repentance does.

See with your mind's eye, think with your heart but learn the difference.

Some can't see; some see selectively; some only see others; some block others from seeing but God sees all!

Some lie: some lie unknowingly; some lie purposefully; some mix truth with lies; Satan is the father of Lies!

Sometimes being right or being wrong isn't good or bad.

Sometimes we won't know our emotional core until someone causes it to surface.

Trust in what you believe not how you feel.

Without faith there can be no trust and without trust faith is Hollow.

I Believe Declaration:

- I am Successful
- I am Victorious
- I am Delivered
- I am Rich
- I am Smart
- I am Strong
- I am Healed
- I am Beautiful
- I am Good
- I am Saved
- I am Protected
- I am Complete
- I am Free
- I am Healthy
- I am Happy
- I am Debt Free
- I am A Home Owner
- I am Covered
- I am Spirit Filled
- I am Sealed
- I am Wise
- I am Intelligent
- I am Powerful
- I am Faithful
- I am an Over comer
- I am Sober
- I am Patient

- I am Kind
- I am Long Suffering
- I am a Giver
- I am a Tither
- I am Focused
- I am Determined
- I am Prepared
- I am Redeemed
- I am Set Free
- I Love God
- I Trust God
- I Trust Jesus
- I Love Jesus

Things I am NOT!

- I am not a failure
- I am not a loser
- I am not captured
- I am not poor
- I am not dumb
- I am not weak
- I am not sick
- I am not ugly
- I am not bad
- I am not Lost
- I am not abandoned
- I am not incomplete
- I am not bound
- I am not sickly
- I am not sad
- I am not in debt
- I am not homeless
- I am not uncovered
- I am not spiritless
- I am not unsealed
- I am not foolish
- I am not stupid
- I am not helpless
- I am not unfaithful
- I am not overcome
- I am not a drunkard
- I am not impatient
- I am not unkind
- I am not devil owned
- I am not unwilling to suffer
- I am not stingy
- I am not a tithe with holder
- I am not a scatterbrain
- I am not uncommitted

- I am not unprepared
- I am not in bondage
- I don't hate God
- I don't doubt God
- I don't hate Jesus
- I don't doubt Jesus

Prayer

A Prayer for Finding what is being Sought

Heavenly Father,

Today I come before Your Throne asking that You bring into captivity all the things that Your Sons and Daughters are seeking. Father God, I am asking that You help each person to be in the right place at the right time with Faith to receive Their reward for what they have been seeking. Do not let their needs to go more day without Your answer or without You giving strength to the feeble. I know that there is not anyway for anyone to find what they are seeking unless You may it available. I know You have the power to cause those invisible things and those things that can't manifest themselves to materialize. I am praying that You have Your Word to perform for us all in this critical time of seeking. When all other attempts have failed and hopelessness has spread like wildfire throughout the land grant your People safe haven into your presence, in Christ's Name. Amen.

A Prayer for those who respect Godliness

Heavenly Father,

Today I come before You with a clear conscience. Thanking You for the righteousness that You have imparted into Human Vessels. I am aware that without Your power and without the spirit we all would remain victims of lustful desires. Therefore, thank You for those who do not want to be weak. And, for those who do not want to yield to the flesh. Father God, I pray that you continue to bless us. And bless those who desire to be Godly and respect Godliness with the fullness of Your deliverance power. I pray that You grant them moments of clarity and of freedom in order for them to accept absolute deliverance. I know that Godliness cannot be attained without Faith and Trust in You. Grant them Lord of power to walk away, to stand up, to turn around and to take power over that which has had power over them for far too long. Lord Jesus, we rest in Your Authority over all the powers in the universe. I believe that You will answer this Prayer in Christ Jesus's Name, Amen.

A Prayer for Those Who know What is being Said

Heavenly Father,

Heavenly Father we pray for all of those who understand that that is not what we are saying! There are those who will twitch our Words. But we are saying in our discussions, in our conversations and we are praying that we all come to the unity of the Faith! Let us now get their ears and always grant us peace and not war in words or in thoughts. And, when those thoughts have been manifested and are in conflict then let their end failure. We know that you are the God of Peace and the God of Reconciliation. We are asking how we help reconcile a world with so many differences. Lord God help us understand how to bring reconciliation, peace, equality, Justice and social well-being to our society. We need you Lord! We need you God! We need you Heavenly Father! And we ask that you do all that is Godly possible to bring about your Earth as it is in Heaven in Jesus's Name Amen!

A Prayer for Our Way Out

Heavenly Father,

I pray this prayer for everyone who is trying to find a way out. I understand that the way out will not be easy. I know that there is a struggle after you have found yourself in and now you trying to get a way out. I thank you Lord God for the revelation that OUT is what's needs to happen for me and for so many! I know that unless we can believe we will stay stuck! Lord, I Thank you for forgiving us and seeing our Faith. Now Heavenly Father, I ask that you booster our trust so no matter what befalls upon us while we are trying to get out and no matter how hopeless it seems, because you have assured us that we will make it out alive and well thank you Lord God. And for all of us that are still locked in prison and in our own self-made bondage give us Freedom for we seek it. I pray for our way out in the mighty name of Jesus! Thank You Father for providing resources and for providing Deliverance with all the help we need in Jesus's Name, Amen!

A Prayer for Scriptural Context

Heavenly Father,

Too many Scriptural Interpretations for Centuries upon Centuries have grown and have been born out of Private Interpretation and not Scriptural Context. However, in these Last Days the need has become more and more abundantly clear that Doctrines have sprung up out of Social Economical Expedient. For Thousands of years Individuals have paid the man of God or people who represented themselves as such to give them a Specific Word. Today People are paying to get a Specific word. Doctrines like the Prosperity Doctrine, Once Saved Always Saved, The No Standard, Same Gender Doctrine and many more! Father God I am praying that you open our eyes and clear our minds. We need to be led by Scriptural Context in our continuation to accomplish Christian Order and Principles in Godly Living in Christ Jesus's Name Amen!

A Prayer to be loosed from Sinful Entanglements

Good Lord my God,

Today I come before You seeking freedom from Sinful Entanglements in my life and the Lives of all who might be entangled. Without Your Liberating power and deliverance there is no way we will be set free! Our needs are Great! Doing wrong is not our heart's desire. Loving You and Pleasing You is. We need You to Guide Us and Direct our footsteps. Help Us now! Lead us up and down the Righteous Paths. Sinful choices are plentiful and in great abundance! We cannot hide because everywhere we turn on the right or on the left Sinful Choices are present. Thank You our Great God and our Great Deliverer in Christ Jesus's Name I PRAY AMEN!

A Prayer for Divine Blessings upon this Home and Property

Heavenly Father

I come before You, Thanking You for Your Blessings. There is no doubt that without both Your mercies and favor this accomplishment would not have occurred. Thank You Lord for the doors that You have opened to make this opportunity possible. Now, Father God, I ask that You bless this building. Bless this House and make it a Home! Bless the foundation, bless the structure, bless the inside and outside and bless the Ground it rests upon. Lord, unless You bless this Property it will fall into the hands of those who would cause damage and harm. Put Your protective hands around and over it. Do not allow bad weather to damage it. Thank You Lord God for blessing the Owner. Keep the Owner financially secure so that this Home, Property and Land will always be a blessing and never a burden. Thank You Lord God and in Christ Jesus's Name Amen!

A Prayer for Usage of Gifts

Lord God,

Thanks for the privilege of being able to come before you. Thank You for the abilities that You have given unto Your People. I pray for the Usage of Gifts and ask that You have them spread joy. I pray that the gifts will not be an instrument of sadness. Let the gifts be used for the purpose for which they were given. I pray that the recipients of your gifts will always be covered by Your hand of mercy, safety and protection. Blessed the Believers to grow and mature spiritually throughout the years. Have Your grace and mercy be their food. Bless them so that they are depended only upon you. Make them to be self-reliant, self-sufficient and righteous! Not only bless them to be careful and safe over the Usage of Gifts but how they share their Gifts as well. Father God, please guide all of Us so that we don't merchandise usage of Our Gifts. Thank you, Lord, in the precious name of Jesus I pray Amen.

A Prayer for the World

Lord Our God,
And God Our Lord,
Heavenly Father,

Without many Words bless the World! Let it and have it
overflow with your Mercy and Grace. There are too many
Needs to list each one. And the list continues to grow.
Without you there is not anything that your People can do to
overcome the World! Our Prayer is that you look favorably
on your creation. We pray that Your will be done! While
our words are limited, We know that your Power is without
comparison. Bless our Faith and bring Your People together
without Doubt standing in Faith upon Your WORD. Send the
living WORD for such a time as this. Father God our Prayer
is that You bless the World in Christ Jesus's Name, Amen!

A Prayer for Prevention of Wrongful Doings

God of GLORY,

You know oh too well of Humanity frailties! On one hand desiring to do right but finding unrighteousness at every turn! Seemingly at every door there is Evil upon Evil. Some Wrongful Doings appears repulsive and yet some Wrongful Doings appears appealing and seductive! Lord Jesus, Man and Mankind is in desperate need of Your saving Power. This Prayer is for Deliverance from Wrongful Doings in all every Man, and Mankind in Christ Jesus's Name I Pray, Amen.

A Prayer for Employment/ Work/Job

Heavenly Father,

Grant favor to all that Seek You for assistance in attaining employment, work or a job opportunities. Let them know that Your desire is for both Male and Female to be able to earn a living. We need You to Bless and Open Up Our Economy. Bless the Employers with resources and supplies so that they need workers. Also, Bless the Employers with Customers and Clients.

Father God, we want Workers to work in safe environments. We need Your protection and Your guidance for all those that seek it. We pray that Your People have a Righteous work ethics. We want Your People to walk in Your attribute of Benevolence. Now, there are too many people who are struggling because they do not have enough Income to pay their bills. We put our trust in your word that states," it is more Blessed to give than to receive". Thank You Father God for filling the pockets of Your People with money. Bless each and every one of them with surpluses so that they all might be givers and not one goes without. Make Your People the head and not the tail! Father God, I know that I have not asked for anything too hard for You in Christ's Name Amen.

A Prayer to Silence the Noise

Father God,

I come before You on behalf of all of Us who are experiencing overwhelming and distracting Noise. We stand in need of having the volume turned down so that we can think clearly. The noise is so disruptive and disturbing that it is blocking the ability to meditate. The power of concentration has been bounded. Father God, you know what evil is being inflicted on Your Children and why we can't get a Prayer through! Help us Now, I pray and block out the Noise in Christ Jesus's Name Amen.

A Prayer for a Better Life

Heavenly Father,

I need your grace in order see better what is a very difficult situation. I need help understanding how to be positive when bad things are mounting up against me. I know that the answer is not only in Victory and that sometimes the answer may be in a change of mind. I need a touch of your kindness, of your goodness and of your Mercies. Help me to understand that a change in mindset is the first step toward a better life. Deliverer me from the power of sadness, depression and self-loathing. Give back to me the Joy of Life gladly celebrating each day with hopefulness. Help me stand firm on your WORD that always encourages me to believe that "All Things Work Together for Good". Father God help me put all my trust in Your WORD in Christ Jesus's Name, Amen!

A Prayer for Joy and Peace

Heavenly Father,

Today I am praying that You to all those that ask and all those that seeks Your Peace. Not only, Your Peace but Your Joy. The Joy that cannot be taken away by the sorrows of this current time. It is clear that this generation is experiencing troubles that hasn't been seen for more the five Generations.

Father God, I am praying that You stabilize our Hearts and Regulate our Minds. Saturate us with Your Spirit! Do not allow hopelessness to conquer our Faith and do not have our Adversary steal our Victory! The devastation of this current time needs to be fixed by the overcoming Resurrection Power of Christ our Lord. Help us to be wise and proactive in our efforts to improve these demoralizing conditions.

Savior I am praying that You feed us with the Truth of Your Word. Shield us from the weakness of our Flesh! Cover us with Your Peace and lead us to the fountain of Your Joy in Christ's Name, Amen.

A Prayer for Renewal

The Lord of both Heaven and Earth, Everlasting
Father and soon coming King,
Hear our prayer we pray thee,

Weakness has prevailed throughout the Land! Continuously,
Wrong choices have been made that are taking Your People off
the righteous path! Too many believers have gravitated to Sin We
are praying for those who are so easily LED astray. Help them so
that they will regain their Religious Compass. Unrighteousness is
walking in and out amongst your people. Up and down even in
the sanctuaries of Worshippers. Today, we pray for renewal We
pray for the church to be refreshed. Help us once again become
strong and spiritual. Rekindle your light, renew your eternal flame
in us and save us. Help us Lord to reclaim our rightful place in
your kingdom. Help us once again to be who you want us to be.
Thank you, Heavenly Father for LOVING us. Thank you, Heavenly
Father for hearing our prayers. And most importantly thank you
Heavenly Father for answering our prayers in Jesus's Name Amen.

A Plea Prayer

Jesus!!!
Help me Jesus!
Help my loved ones, help my family, help my
friends, and help all those who seek after you.
Lord Jesus Christ!
Lord Jesus!
Help;
Father God, my plea right now is I need thee! My family need
thee, my friends need thee, and the world needs thee!
Help, help us all in the name of Jesus I pray, Amen.

A Prayer for Help!

Lord God and Heavenly Father,

Lord help me to separate, disconnect from wrongdoing
and doers of wrong from this day forward:

Lord bless my family, friends, loved ones and all those
that looks unto you as their helper for food, shelter,
wellness, spiritual growth and financial prosperity!

Lord grant me wisdom, awareness, insight and
knowledge to manage, avoid, escape, and be delivered
from all that desires to seek out and kill, steal or
destroy me, my family, friends and loved ones:

Lord expose, reveal and make visible the actions of all those
who seek profit, financial gain, division, hatred and continual
oppression of the vulnerable, weak, and the defenseless.

Lord for the hurt, the sick, the depressed, the lost,
and the forgotten I pray you comfort them. I pray that
you release from your unlimited supplies, healing,
mercy and grace to minster to all needs:

Lord, please stop the division that is running rampant
in the Body of Christ causing one to be against the
other in unrighteousness, self-righteousness
and self-serving dogma:

Lord, I pray that you give sight to our blinded eyes that we all may see; that you open our blocked ears so that we all may hear; Lord heal our lameness so that we all might walk in your light:

Lord, I pray that my mess up do not destroy my setup; Lord, my most earnest prayer is that you to bind the weapons of the enemy so that they do not prevail. And, have those who desire to be free and who seek to be free be freed by the power of Christ.

Lord, I pray for those that have more than enough and that they be willing givers to those that have needs; Let their giving be directed by you and guided by hospitality in Christ Jesus's name, Amen.

A Prayer for Help in Making the Right Decision

Heavenly Father,

There is a flood of choices all having backers claiming they are the right choice. So many People rightly have place stock in what they were told. People are looking for accurate and good information. So, it seems most appropriate to TRUST and RELY on the Experts. Sadly, there's contradictory information being dissimulated by the Experts. Father God, this is why in the CHURCH so many Doctrines stands! Thank You Father for Grace and Mercy.

A Prayer for moving Beyond Our Circles

Heavenly Father,

First, we thank You for our Circles of Families, Friends and Loved Ones. With great appreciation we acknowledge the incalculable value of their contributions to our success.

We are confident that we must move beyond our Circles if we are to impact the World. Help us to be both open and receptive to others. Help us to be proactive and not just reactive.

Place us at the intersection of lives so that we may interface with those who are seeking You. Let our lives be fully directed by Your Spirit! Father God, widen our circles. Help us to be effective in the World for Thy Kingdom. Remove us from the place of complacency! Increase our sense of urgency and have compassion be our motivation.

Father Almighty, we pray that Your People move into a continual and perpetual state of expansion. Saturate us with Your Power. We need washing and cleansing from our biases and prejudices. Deliver us so that we are not judgmental of People You call.

Lord God, save such as should be saved in Christ Jesus' Name we Pray, Amen.

A Prayer of Thanks for YOU GOD.

Gracious God and Heavenly Father,

Thank You for being God! Thank You for being Father God! Thank You for being Savior God and thank You for being my God!

Lord God, I thank You for being You. For you are Good and not Evil; For You are Kind and not Selfish; For You are Merciful and not Revengeful; For You are Loving and not Hateful; For You are Righteous and not unrighteous; For You are Just and not Unjust; Yes, Lord God, You are all Holy and absolutely nothing Unholy.

Lord, I thank You for Your Spirit. I thank You for pouring Your Spirit into my Heart. I thank You for Regeneration, New Birth and the Saving of my Soul. I thank You for being the only True and Living God. For being God Almighty and Our Everlasting Father with no Equal.

Lord Jesus, I thank you! I thank You for Your Redemptive Work at Calvary. Today, I thank You for being my Comforter. For being my Peace, my Joy and my Salvation.

Father God, today, tomorrow and forever. I thank You with my lips, my tongue, my breathe, with my mind, with my whole heart and with my worship! Father I pray that all People see You as You are in Christ Jesus Name, Amen!

A Prayer of Thanks for Special People

Father God,

There are many People for whom I am thankful for. And it is because of Your Goodness that these Individuals have been in my Life. I thank You for my parents, my siblings, my spouse, my children, my grandchildren, my aunts and uncles, my cousins, my nephews and nieces, my grandparents and my Great-grandparents, etc., I am thankful for adoptive families and guardians. And I am thankful for my friends, acquaintances and colleagues.

Lord God, I am thankful for my church family and kingdom sisters and brothers. I know that this is not a comprehensive list of people that I am thankful for. Truly, there are a lot of people responsible for helping me in things big and small in my life. And there are too many of them for me to name Individually but I thank You for each and every one of them.

Father God, I thank You for those People that You placed in my life to correct my path. For those whom have poured Word and Wisdom into me. Most of all, I thank You for Your Son Christ Jesus. I thank You for the work he did on Calvary that reconciled me to You.

Lord God, I pray for healing of relationships where sicknesses exist. I pray for unity in homes where division exist. And I pray for growth of families, friends and love ones Thanks Father God, thank You and in Christ's Name I pray Your will be done, Amen...

A Prayer Thanking God for Differences

Heavenly Father,

Thank You Father God for diversity in the Human Race. Thank You for all the different Groups, Tongues and Cultures.

Thank You for the rainbow of Colors. More importantly, Lord thanks for bringing us to realize that Your creative differences are Gifts to the Human Race to be appreciated. Help each of us to recognize the beauty of our various heights, sizes, weights and pigmentation.

Thank You Lord for all those who see Your handiwork as blessings. For we know the need exist for all of us to work towards Unity in preaching, teaching and living. Lord, we are aware that thousands of years have passed, and Humanity has not changed its patterns in terms of living together or coexisting.

We know that the seeds of hatred and mistrust have been planted in the DNA of man's Spirit. Without You Lord, without Your help we will continue on this path of Intolerance and Racial and Ethnic Hatred.

We thank You for enlightenment and togetherness. We bless Your Name for leading us out of darkness. We pray that You lead Your creation into Your Kingdom in Christ's Name, Amen.

A Special Prayer of Thanksgiving

Heavenly Father,

Today we opened our eyes to new challenges and opportunities. Thank You for this Day. We know that Your Grace is always available, and we thank You.

When everything is gone, Heavenly Father, we with unwavering gratitude Thank You. Knowing You are with us in the darkness of our nights we thank You. For those who have been spared sadness, emptiness and loneliness we Thank You. For those who have more than enough we thank You. For those who are without food and shelter but still trust You we thank You. For those whose cups runs over with Compassion we thank You. For those who come to believe in Christ Jesus our Savior we thank You.

Father, God, we trust You. We believe that nothing in this present time has nor can derail Your plan. We pray that Your Mercy and Favor continues to encompass us in Jesus's Name, Amen.

A Special Prayer
Addition of Thanks

HEAVENLY FATHER,

I am praying from a place of perpetual need.
And, while my needs still exist, I want to thank You for being
mindful of me. Just knowing that You have not forgotten me
or overlooked me encourages me to continue in Faith.

I know that through this transitional period disappointments will
happen. So, I thank You for helping me to understand that our
relationship is not based on what You do in answering my prayers.

For I accept knowing that all my prayers will not
be answered. I accept not my will but thine will be
done. I know You know what is best for me.

Thank You Father for keeping me from the attitude of doubt
and mistrust. I thank You for helping me understand that
my continual life after this life is over is in Your hands.

Father God, thank You in Christ's Name I pray Amen.

An Intuitive Prayer

Heavenly Father,

Today Lord I come unto You praying for the Ears of all those who come in contact with Your Word. I know that there are forces attempting to block the message and plug the Ears of all those who would hear. These forces do not want people to hear and respond in Faith and Obey. There are Disciples who wittingly or unwillingly do the bidding of the Deceiver. They devise messages to MISLEAD and CONTROL all who are Vulnerable and susceptible. I am praying for everyone that has a predisposition and have viable receptors to be Misled and Controlled.

Father God, Your Word informs us of both the power and scope of DECEPTION. My Prayer is that You provide and give all who will wear the Helmet of SALVATION. Protect our Minds from lies, falsehoods and partial truths.

Lord God, too many People are choosing Evil and Evil Devices over Good and Light. Help Your People and the Harvest in this greatest season of Spiritual Darkness. As You have Sealed Your Children with Your Spirit also expose Evil and Wickedness that has put on disguises of Goodness.

Hate, hate and hate is the main course of so many meals. Day in and Day out on the right and on the left HATE is being digested. Even more sadly, Children of all ages, of all Nationalities, of all Races, and of all colors are being fed HATE.

Children are developing and appetite for hatred and they are being taught that hate is necessary. Hate has already been dressed and clothed in Silk and Cashmere. I am praying for what cannot be seen on the horizon. I am praying for Peace, Unity, and Love in Our Lord Jesus Christ Name, Amen.

A Prayer for Strengthen of Weakened Faith

Heavenly Father,

Thank You for hearing my prayer. Today I come before You on behalf of all Believers whose Faith have been negatively impacted by current Life Troubles. For many Believers are confronting extreme challenges hindering Their Faith from staying afloat. Too many Families are hurting; Too many are trying to survive and overcome sickness, hunger, homelessness and death while barely holding to hope. Therefore, Lord of God, I am praying that You send a Word of Encouragement, a Sign of Encouragement, and an Act of Encouragement to Strengthens Weakened Faith. I know You will feed our Faith. But still division is growing in the Body. One Group is believing one thing while another Group is believing another thing and yet another Group is believing another thing so forth and so on. We know Your Word calls for UNITY of the Faith, so I pray that You send a unifying Word, a Fresh Word to Convict and Convert our Hearts. As a Song Writer wrote, "Draw us Lord Precious Lord closer to Thee." Father God, I pray that Your will be done amongst Your People all over the Earth. In Jesus Christ's Name I pray Amen...

A Prayer for Acceptance

Heavenly Father,

Thank You for not abandoning the Human Race. Thank You for giving us a second chance and a third chance and after that chance a chance after that. Thank You for making us the Heart Your Creations. This Week on the planet Earth in the World of Humanity especially in these United States we really need You. Many atrocities have happened throughout the centuries and the millennium where People have lost their way. We here in these United States are on the verge of chaos, disaster, conflict, and unspeakable tragedies. We need a bridge, a hand of Deliverance, a way of avoidance and away of escape to keep us from certain destruction.

Father God, we need you to step in and bridge the gap between the Right and Left and between the Red and Blue. Your children on both sides are fighting amongst themselves claiming to be in line with Your WILL.

Father our God, we need you to allow your spirit to flourish, minister, sew together the tear in the body. Help us now that we may be representatives of Your Glory, of One Faith, of One Baptism and all in One Body. In the Name of Christ Jesus, I pray Amen.

A Prayer for Spiritual Sight

Heavenly Father,

I come before You Today praying for Spiritual Sight. For there are too many Evils Forces going undetected until they have accomplished their objectives. Lord Jesus, Your People need to be able to detect the Evil at its genesis stage of formation before it is planted and have had time to germinate and grow. Lord God, we are praying that You help of utilize the Gift of Spiritual Knowledge to understand the development and course of a thang before it occurs. We need to be able to see what the end is going to be. So much of Evil is dressed up to look good and to sound good only, as a way, to appeal to our Natural being. It is clear, that appeal is counterproductive to our Well Being and our Salvation. The glitter blinds our spiritual receptors and make us vulnerable to the evil that is within and behind the glitter. Father, we need You! Help me to see The ME. Help the Me to see the Me so that I can stop Evil from being a Passenger in my daily walk. Help every Me get clear sight so that Evil is STOP. And Lord every Me need to be WOKE and SEE. In the exalted Name of Jesus Christ I pray, Amen.

A Prayer for Needs

Heavenly Father,

The World needs Your Wisdom; The World requires Your Guidance; The World needs Your Leadership; The World needs Your Peace; The World needs Your Healing; The World needs Your Righteousness; Release Your You; The Church needs more of Your Holy Spirit; Your People needs more of Your Righteousness; More of Your Kindness, More of Love, More of Your Forgiveness, and More of Your Goodness; Bless all who welcome a double portion of Your Spirit. Father, I ask now for Healing of and from Division in the Faith. Please provide Oneness and Singleness of Belief in Righteousness and Faith. Cast down with Fierceness Self Righteousness and reclothe Your Children in Holiness. Have the Light of Your Word expose Deception. Cut out Greed from amongst Your People. Water the Soil of the Hearts of Your Sons and Daughters so that the Fruit of Your Spirit Grows. In Christ's Mighty Name I Pray, Amen.

A Prayer for Churches Answers

Heavenly Father,

I come before you seeking the understanding that is needed for your People in this moment. I am asking for You to give the Words that You would have us speak in this moment. Lord, looking at the State of Affairs in your House with some People fearing to return because of the CORONAVIRUS 19. Father, so many Believers, even in this hour, need direction from You about the work that You would have done. We need to hear from you! We need your guidance! Father, if we are to accomplish the mission, You would have us to accomplish, in this earth, we need to hear from you. Father, if we need to be quiet so that we can hear lead us to a quiet place. If we need to be on our knees in prayer and travail, Father, direct us and meet us in prayer. Lord, I know that there is work still to be done. Souls still need to be saved. Sick Folk still need to be healed. Evil in the land still need to be removed. So, we look to You Lord the Author and Finisher of our Faith. Help us in this darkest of hours to rise up and be the Church of light in this dark World. Help us lead the Lost to Salvation! In the precious Name of Jesus I Pray, Amen.

A Prayer for Your Perspective

Heavenly Father,

Thank You for the invitation to come before your
Throne. Father God, there are Millions of People with
Millions of Perspectives. Some Perspectives seem more
reasonable than others. Some Perspectives seem
more plausible than others. And some Perspectives
seem right while others seem wrong. But, whatever
the case maybe, I am praying that You bring all
Believers in alignment with Your Perspective.

Lord, there is, as it seems, a hierarchy of Perspectives based
solely on whose Perspective it is. It is clear to me that the Devil is
and has been making monumental strides in pitting Perspectives
at odds one against the other. Some display their Perspectives
as Banners. Some have attached negative stigma to differing
perspectives purely because of their interpretational judgment.

Father, I am asking that You open the minds and hearts of
Your People. Help us to understand that it was You that
established Your Kingdom on Earth amongst Earthly Kingdoms.
You required that Your members be in the World but not of
the World. Again, Father God, the craftiness of the Devil has
drawn Millions of Your People in a conflict between Believers
based on Godliness verses Love, based on Interpretation verses
Interpretation and Perspectives verses Perspectives. We truly

need Your help Lord in straighten Your People out. Help us to see clearly, Sin! Help us to understand that Laws and Lawmakers are for the Kingdoms of the World. But Your Kingdom Governance is by the Righteousness of Christ, Your Word and the Holy Spirit. Teach us how to Pray for the Lawmakers and Leaders of the World. Please Lord order the steps of Your Kingdom Leadership. Bless them to be of one voice and unified. Bless all who name the Name of Christ as Lord and Savior get out of the way and allow Jesus to Shine Forth. Lord, help all of us to see Our Failures. Help all of us to confront Our short comings. And, Father, accept Our repentance for all have Sin that causes us to come short of Your Glory. In the Name of Christ Jesus I Pray, Amen.

A Prayer about Coronavirus 19

Heavenly Father,

I humbly come before your throne seeking mercy during this worldwide Coronavirus Pandemic. The need for a cure is great. And the need for treatments is equally as great. Therefore, I am praying like many are all around the World that You Led, Guide and Direct those looking and seeking for Cures and Treatments to discover them. I am praying for the MIRACLE of Treatments and Cures. In the meantime, I am praying that You provide Safety from the Virus for as many as are seeking it. Help keep us mindful of the things to avoid, of the places to go and not go and being in compliance with all the things that help us. Now, if we do contract the Virus, I pray that You strengthen our bodies so that the infection is so mild that there aren't any negative effects. But if there are negative effects do not allow them to be unto death. Do not let it cause long lasting debilitating conditions. Lord, tens of thousands have already died as a result of contracting COVID 19 and countless thousands more have been severely sickened. Lord, You are needed in the sickness and You are needed in the pain. I am praying for Comfort for all who are impacted by this Pandemic.

Father God, for Your Children, Your Sons and Daughters that are sick unto death I pray that You give them You PEACE that surpasses Understanding. Give them a reassuring JOY that casts out Fear and gladness because the Battle is over. With OVERCOMING power help us accept Your will in the Name of Jesus Christ, Amen.

A Prayer for Restoration

Heavenly Father,
Merciful and Forgiving God,

I come before you with a heavy heart. Seeking forgiveness for the wrongdoing of Your People. They have allowed Idolatry and Greed to take residence in their Minds. Their thoughts have become impure continually. Their conversations are Unholy and Unsanctified.

Heavenly Father,

I ask that you wash their minds with the Holy Spirit. That You Purify and Lift their thoughts and give them direction with a New Focus. I pray that You Restore Your People. I pray that You revive Your People and deliver them from themselves and keep them Safe from Others. Lord, I ask that You Cover, Forgive and Restore all Your People. In the Name of Jesus I pray, Amen.

A Prayer for Spiritual Activities

Heavenly Father,
Eternal and Almighty God,
Praise be unto Your Holy Name.

In prayer I come before you I thank you for your Goodness to all believers and non-believers alike. I ask that You use this pandemic as an Instrument in Your service to bring about a great Harvest. I call upon You to have Your Mercy and Compassion become visible and evident in these troubled Days. I asked for miracles to be birth everywhere all around the World. And, that a Cure be discovered to fight back the sicknesses of COVID 19. Activate the word of knowledge and wisdom in those enlisted in Your service. Lord Jesus, please let Your Spirit spring forth like rivers of Living Water. Release Your blessings and let them flow beyond our greatest expectation. Fix and repair relationships, deliver the addicts, strengthen the mind of those contemplating suicide, blessed the hungry with food and the homeless with shelter. Thank You Father God for all that You do. Thank You Father for blessing the World through Jesus Christ our Lord, Amen.

A Prayer for Believers

Heavenly Father,

Today is a day of contemplation, a day of reflection, a day of meditation, a day of questioning, a day of searching and a day of seeking. Father God, today so many of Your Sons and Daughters aren't attending Church. Their attendance has been put on pause due to COVID 19 restrictions and not because they have forsaken Your HOUSE. Many of Your children are questioning if they will ever be able to return to CHURCH. Death, sickness, fear and financial woes has caused all kinds of Misery. The Body of Christ hasn't received an exemption nor a pass from the NEGATIVE IMPACT of COVID 19. COVID 19 has with great destruction affected Believers of every FAITH and the World at large. With no end in sight for healing, comfort and emotional relief many are desperately seeking someone to blame.

Father God, even within the Body of Christ some have assigned the blame to You as punishment for SINS of the Church or Sins of the World at large. Lord, this I do know and that is Places of Worship all over this World have Paused. And this I believe that even this is going to work out for our GOOD. Therefore, strip each and every one of us of the things that need to be let go. Mold and shape us into the People You want us to become. Lord, I pray that You grant Your People reassurance that they are safe and secure in Your Everlasting Arms. Provide them with reassurance that nothing can separate them from Your Love. And Father God lead us through these perilous times in the precious Name of Jesus, Amen.

A Prayer for Strength to Change

Father God,

I pray that you allowed change to come into my life. I ask that You bring change into my life. I need You to help me use this time for self-examination. Help me use this time wisely for an introspective search.

Lord, I thank you for leading me to the awareness that my life needs to change. Thank you for awakening me to the reality that I have been wasting time. I have been under utilizing my potential. I have been abusing and misusing my abilities. I have misused my time for the purpose of doing wrong. I have allowed my time to be used to cause hurt, to cause pain, and to bring about destruction in others' lives. Lord Jesus, I have brought it about in my own life, please deliver me. In your Name I pray, Amen!

A Prayer for The Lost

Heavenly Father,
Creator of Life and Lover of Our Souls!

Today I come before Your Throne of Mercy asking that You rescue the Lost. So many Individuals have not found their way into Your Loving Arms. So many are still bond by the Power of Darkness. These are People of every Race, Creed and Nationality! Some of these Individuals may have heard of Your Redemptive Love and have yet to respond. Some may still be unaware of Calvary's Work. And, yes, some may have found their way and lost it again. No matter the case today I ask You to do what only what You can do. Save Lord Save! Lord Save the Lost! In Christ Jesus' Name Amen!

A Prayer for Marriages

Father God,
God Of Heaven,
Hear me I pray for you,

Many marriages have entered very troubled times. The love
that apparently brought couples together has been lost,
destroyed or stolen. Instead of talking they are fighting and
sleeping apart. The Children are caught in the middle. Lord I
pray that you touch their hearts and minds. Touch them that
they may find love again and have it fill their hearts. I ask that
you will step in and save their marriages. Please do not let them
forsake the bond that they once shared. Open their eyes, help
them get control and not be victims to their intolerance of one
another. I ask that you work through the Holy Spirit and keep
violent out of their marriages. Lord I pray that you hear this
prayer and send them healing and send them Deliverance. Bless
them together with sustaining victory. Bless them with stress-
free conversation and give them moments of clarity. Bless their
marriage with forgiveness and healing. What you have joined
together do not let anything destroy it. In Jesus Name Amen.

Prayer Diary

Prayer for Your Spiritual Growth

Prayer for Your Children/Child

Prayer for Your Success

Prayer for Your Best Life

Prayer for Your Deliverance

Prayer for Your Family

Printed in the United States
by Baker & Taylor Publisher Services